HELP FOR A COMPLEX SYNDROME

Mitral valve prolapse (MVP) affects nearly seven million Americans, yet conventional medicine has no remedy for this common benign valvular disorder.

In this original new look at MVP, a leading doctor of nutritional medicine examines the wide-ranging array of seemingly unrelated symptoms that sometimes accompany this syndrome—from shortness of breath to panic attacks, from feeling "wired but tired" to heart palpitations—and comes up with a theory that links them all together. Then he offers natural health-enhancing ways to alleviate the symptoms including dietary changes, vitamin and mineral supplementation, herbal relaxants, exercise and meditation techniques.

ABOUT THE AUTHOR

Ronald L. Hoffman, M.D., is Medical Director of The Hoffman Center in New York City. A graduate of Albert Einstein College of Medicine, he is a Diplomate of the American College for Advancement of Medicine and The American Academy of Environmental Medicine. He is the author of *Lyme Disease* (A Keats Good Health Guide), *The Diet-Type Weight Loss Program, Seven Weeks to a Settled Stomach* and *Tired All the Time: How to Regain Your Lost Energy.* He also hosts "Health Talk," a daily radio program which is syndicated nationally.

Natural Therapies for Mitral Valve Prolapse

How diet and nutritional supplements can ease the symptoms of this common disorder

Ronald L. Hoffman, M.D.
Author of *Lyme Disease*

Keats Publishing, Inc.  New Canaan, Connecticut

Natural Therapies for Mitral Valve Prolapse is not intended as medical advice. Its intent is solely informational and educational. Please consult a health professional should the need for one be indicated.

Contents

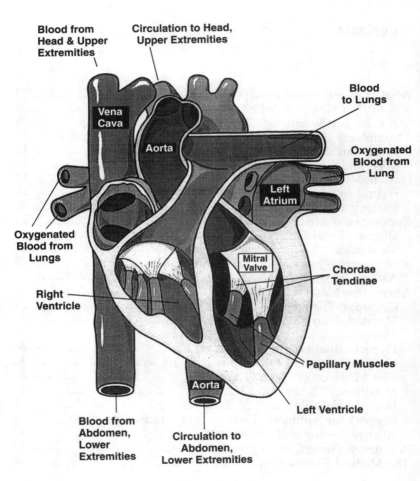

Figure 1
Anatomy of the Heart

WHAT IS MITRAL VALVE PROLAPSE?

Mitral valve prolapse (MVP) is a fairly common medical problem that is the focus of some controversy and even confusion among both physicians and those who suffer from it. There is both less to this syndrome and more to it than at first appears. Mitral valve prolapse is named for a heart valve and is usually first diagnosed as a faint heart "click" or murmur, though it isn't a form of heart "disease" in any conventional sense. It is a relatively benign condition, though it is linked to a confusing array of seemingly unrelated symptoms from shortness of breath to panic attacks. Mitral valve prolapse is generally the most benign of the various types of heart murmurs and is probably genetic in origin. It is the most common valvular disorder in the industrialized nations at present since the risk of heart murmurs from rheumatic fever has been reduced. Mitral valve prolapse is thought to affect 5 percent of the population or nearly seven million people, though the number of borderline cases may be much higher.

The Mitral Valve

The mitral valve is a valve of the heart (see Figure 1). Its function is to keep the blood flowing in one direction through the left side of the heart and to prevent backflow of blood when the heart contracts. It is named for its shape, which resembles a tall bishop's hat called a miter. It is made up of two triangular-shaped, leaf-like fibrous membranes, thin but tough, which are attached to strong cords like parachute cords, in turn attached to muscles. When the heart contracts, the two membranes or leaves billow up to close off the opening between the upper atrium and the lower ventricle on the left side of the heart. "Prolapse" means that the two leaves are a little loose, a little floppy, so that the valve doesn't close as firmly as it might. It may close with a faint click or may permit a tiny amount of blood to leak through, producing a heart murmur.

For decades doctors who listened to their patients' hearts with a stethoscope would sometimes hear the faint clicks, but they thought they came from outside the heart, from the heart's movement within the chest cavity. It wasn't until the 60s that a few researchers identified the clicks as coming from the mitral valve. This was partly thanks to a new diagnostic tool, the echocardiogram, which uses ultrasound waves to draw a picture of the interior of the living heart.

IS MVP A HEART PROBLEM?

Though mitral valve prolapse was first identified as an anatomical abnormality of the heart, it is not simply a heart disease in the conventional sense. Cardiologists are beginning to look at this disorder not as a single variation of heart anatomy, but as a whole spectrum of abnormalities, many benign and harmless, but some troubling. Curiously, most of the abnormalities seem related to an underlying instability of the autonomic nervous system. This is the part of our nervous system that regulates the internal visceral functions of the body—such as blood pressure, heart rate, sweating, body temperature, gastrointestinal activity and emptying of the urinary bladder. The autonomic nervous system is directly wired to the adrenal glands and can signal the release of adrenal hormones into the bloodstream. It controls our internal visceral sense of well-being and can move us in seconds from a sleepy, relaxed after-dinner repose to an alert, energized, "fight or flight" condition in response to a surprise or perceived danger.

A COMPLEX SYNDROME

People with mitral valve prolapse seem somehow to be wired differently. Their autonomic response can be much more volatile and unstable, as if set on a hair-trigger, so that normal stresses and surprises set off an exaggerated response, flooding their systems with stress hormones called the catecholamines. In fact, there may not be a specific stressor—autonomic fluxes may occur unpredictably like internal weather changes. In some ways this could be defined as a catecholamine disorder. The principal catecholamines are epinephrine and nor-epinephrine; in Britain they are called adrenaline and nor-adrenaline. People with mitral valve prolapse are intermittently and unpredictably awash in their own catecholamines. This leaves them alternately excited and exhausted; "wired but tired" is a common feeling.

Epinephrine and nor-epinephrine are the hormones that prime the body for a powerful response to danger, sometimes called the "fight or flight" response. They arouse the sympathetic nervous system, which stimulates the body into action and alertness. They cause increased blood pressure, dry mouth, cold hands and feet, butterflies in the stomach and a readiness to leap into action. All these changes can take place in literally seconds. Blood flow floods the primary muscles of the legs and moves away from the extremities. There is an evolutionary explanation for this: animals in combat or flight may have their extremities wounded, and the decrease in blood flow minimizes further damage and loss of blood. All of these changes emanate from the sympathetic nervous system, the counterpart to the parasympathetic system which is associated with relaxation, salivation, digestive processes, sleep and sexual arousal.

If your sympathetic system is aroused, you can suddenly feel crushing chest pain with your heartbeat racing and pounding. You may begin to hyperventilate, feel short of breath and break out into a cold sweat. Certain people with mitral valve prolapse sometimes experience this with no apparent warning or immediate threat. There can be sensations of chest pain, a feeling of doom or detachment, a fear of dying or a desire to flee. If you don't know why this is happening, the symptoms themselves are scary, and the fear of the unknown can prompt an even greater release of stress hormones, driving you into a kind of meltdown of the autonomic nervous system that we call a panic attack.

A panic attack is an intense, visceral and frightening experience, and the sensations can easily be confused with those of a heart attack. Emergency room physicians see a great number of people who come in believing that they are having a heart attack when they are actually experiencing a panic attack. Once people experience this, they generally have a persistent fear of having another attack, which puts them on alert, ready to respond to the slightest symptoms by releasing the very stress hormones that induce panic attacks, thus escalating a new attack.

Since the autonomic nervous system also regulates the churning activity of the stomach, the release of gastrointestinal secretions and contractions of the intestine, autonomic disturbances can create a whole spectrum of weird gastrointestinal symptoms as well. Finally, constant overload with catecholamines appears to affect the immune system, heightening the potential for allergic reactions and causing exaggerated reactions to normal infectious challenges. Most people, including many doctors, don't quite know what to make of this array of seemingly unrelated symptoms and don't associate them with mitral valve prolapse. They can be troubling to experience in themselves and over time become chronic problems, seemingly without solution.

It may seem odd that all of these symptoms should be somehow related to a heart abnormality. In fact, it's not that the mitral valve abnormality causes these other symptoms, but it is a physical trait that is a marker of the underlying condition. Similarly, people with a hyperactive thyroid may have slightly bulging eyes, but this is a physical and diagnostic marker, not the cause of the underlying problem. Like mitral valve prolapse, hyperthyroidism is a condition with a pervasive set of symptoms affecting many body systems. But the eye characteristics are not the problem itself. So it is with mitral valve prolapse. The valve abnormality may be spotted first and is the name given to the syndrome, but we are now beginning to be able to identify the underlying problem that is manifested in other ways as well.

This can be a hard concept for people to grasp, and the medical profession is only gradually coming around to accept it. In fact, many physicians still don't. Because of the way that the syndrome was first identified historically, there's a persistent tendency to look on it simply as a relatively benign heart problem. The fact is, the heart murmur is really just the tip of the iceberg. The mitral valve prolapse is the signature of an underlying instability of the autonomic nervous system. When mitral valve prolapse is diagnosed, we really need to turn our attention to the underlying condition which can cause other disturbing and seemingly unrelated symptoms. The good news is, once we've identified it for what it is, we can effectively manage the condition as well as the symptoms.

Unfortunately not every physician is attuned to this. If you go to your doctor and he hears the murmur, he'll probably do an echocardiogram to confirm it. He may then tell you, "Well, you have this condition called mitral valve prolapse. But don't worry about it, it's not a serious heart problem. It's basically benign. Oh, there's just one thing, you'll need to take a course of antibiotics whenever you have any dental work done just to protect against the possibility of endocarditis. If you do that, you'll be fine."

But there's more to MVP than this. (And more on the antibiotics later.) Your doctor should say: "This is a marker that may indicate that you are susceptible to instabilities of the autonomic nervous system, and you should be aware of some of the possible symptoms and sensitivities. Fortunately, there are preventive strategies you can invoke to avoid some of these problems. Now that we know you have this condition, here are the guidelines on how to cope with it."

SYMPTOMS OF MVP

Instability of the autonomic nervous system can cause or influence a dizzying variety of seemingly unrelated symptoms and conditions affecting many different systems of the body. These include:

- Migraine headaches
- Dizzy, spacey feeling
- Difficulty concentrating
- Balance problems, vertigo
- Insomnia, sleep disturbances
- Hyperventilation, shortness of breath
- Palpitations of the heart, skipped or irregular heartbeat
- Panic attacks with pounding heartbeat
- Phantom chest pain with no apparent physiological cause
- Hypersensitive startled reflex
- Cold sweats

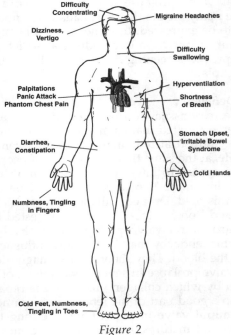

Figure 2
Symptoms of MVP

- Cold hands and feet
- Numbness or tingling in the fingers or toes
- Gastrointestinal upset, irritable bowel syndrome
- Bowel urgency, diarrhea, constipation
- Sensitivity to drugs, including alcohol, caffeine and medications

People with mitral valve prolapse are especially sensitive to all kinds of drugs and medications. For example, caffeine and the theobromides in chocolate prevent the natural absorption of catecholamines so that they linger in the body. Beta blockers, which are used to combat high blood pressure or palpitations, can make those with MVP feel very dizzy and spacey. Dental anesthetics and decongestants, which contain epinephrine or drugs with similar effects, can induce chest sensations, shortness of breath and all kinds of bothersome symptoms.

WHAT CAUSES MVP?

While mitral valve prolapse appears to have a clear genetic basis, there are many factors that may cause the underlying genetic susceptibility to be expressed. In some ways, this might be considered an ailment of our advanced industrial society, and not just because of improved screening and testing. There are several factors that can explain this.

Magnesium Deficiency

One of these reasons has to do with endemic magnesium deficiency. It's been estimated that as much as 40 percent of the population of the industrialized nations suffer from magnesium deficiency while, at the same time, 85 percent of people with mitral valve prolapse appear to have some magnesium deficiency. This begins to look like more than a coincidence. One of the leading researchers in this field, Dr. Leo Galland, along with his colleagues Sidney Baker and Robert McLellan, have suggested that while the tendency toward mitral valve prolapse is probably genetic, the expression of this tendency may be strongly influenced by magnesium levels in the blood. They theorize that magnesium deficiency affects mitral valve prolapse in several ways. First of all, it hinders the mechanism by which collagen grows and is repaired, and collagen makes up a good part of the tendon-like "parachute strings" that hold the mitral valve in place. Over the long term, as heart tissue develops and matures, magnesium deficiency may cause a change in tone of the connective tissue, resulting in a floppy mitral valve along with the other autonomic symptoms. Further, magnesium deficiency increases the level of circulating catecholamines, predisposes to heart arrhythmias and contributes to disregulation of the immune system and the autonomic nervous system. These are all effects that will reinforce symptoms of mitral valve prolapse. As you'd expect, Galland notes that magnesium therapy does seem to relieve the symptoms of mitral valve prolapse.

It may be that other influences, such as the increasing pollution and chemical exposure in industrialized nations, may also affect collagen development, contributing to the expression of innate genetic tendencies.

Our Frenetic Environment

Another factor that may be influencing the increased incidence of mitral valve prolapse is our social environment. Let's face it, this is a society of adrenaline junkies. We use stimulants to wake us up in the morning, then pump ourselves up with more coffee plus deadlines and social interactions on the job; we stimulate ourselves with exciting entertainment events in our free time to fend off depression and boredom. When we go to sports events, to the movies or to concerts, we want to get "a rush." Our movies are laced with violence that is visceral beyond belief, with roller coaster rides of special effects to the point where our hearts are pounding. We rarely sit quietly in our homes at night; the stereo or the television is usually blaring. To some extent, the development of autonomic dysfunction may be the ultimate consequence of a society hooked on catecholamines. Our addiction to stimulants and stimulation may result in a disregulation or burning out of our autonomic system, exacerbating symptoms in susceptible MVP sufferers, though it doesn't, of course, cause the structural MVP abnormality.

Our very foods, from caffeinated soft drinks to high-sugar, high-carbohydrate muffins and pasta contribute to waves of catecholamine release. Sugar and carbohydrate snacking take a tremendous toll on the body's metabolic machinery by triggering fatiguing surges of insulin and counteractive stress hormones. We like the blood sugar highs derived from carbohydrates, but when the blood sugar subsequently bottoms out it calls for a massive release of catecholamines. We are hammering our autonomic nervous systems from all sides with both external and internal stressors. In contrast, someone who lives in a pastoral, environmentally cleaner, slower-paced society and who eats a low-sugar, high-protein diet would be much less likely to experience symptoms from the underlying genetic condition of mitral valve prolapse.

What Can Trigger an Autonomic Response?

Various systemic health problems and imbalances can act as triggers that set off or amplify the autonomic instability. These include:

- Hypoglycemia
- Adrenal instability: hyperactivity followed by adrenal exhaustion
- Hyperthyroidism
- Chemical sensitivities
- Food reactions
- Fluctuating sex hormones, especially estrogen, causing worsened symptoms of PMS and menopause
- Magnesium deficiency
- Increased weakness from virally caused fever; lingering post-viral weakness

People with mitral valve prolapse are a little more feeble immunologically, a little more susceptible to infections and have worse reactions and symptoms when they do become ill. They may normally be active, hard-driving folks, but can suddenly develop a flu that they can't quite shake or experience lingering exhaustion with disturbing symptoms, since the cytokines released by the immune system definitely affect the mind and consciousness.

MVP AND CONDITIONED PSYCHIATRIC DISORDERS

Mitral valve prolapse is not in itself a psychiatric disorder, but it can trigger or amplify psychiatric responses. For example, many people with mitral valve prolapse suffer from phobias. How is this possible? Over time, the repetition of disturbing autonomic symptoms can cause a sort of feedback loop that can worsen and amplify the symptoms. People begin to anticipate the symptoms with dread and associate them with the specific situations that initially aroused them. People with this built-in condition of heightened nervous sensitivity will have "meltdown" experiences that manifest themselves as panic attacks. They will then start to avoid the settings where these occurred and may start to develop phobias. They can easily become agoraphobic, afraid to go out in public. They may become so fearful of having a panic attack that as soon as a mild symptom, such as an increased heart rate, occurs, the fear and anticipation cause it to cascade into a full-fledged attack.

HOW IS MITRAL VALVE PROLAPSE DIAGNOSED?

Women are far more likely than men to be diagnosed with mitral valve prolapse, and oddly, there is even a typical body type. The typical profile is a slender young female with long, tapering fingers, a wide hand span, and a model's figure. They also tend to be especially limber or loose-jointed. Men can have the condition, as can people with a different physique, but the majority of the MVP patients I see fit the standard profile. The condition tends to get picked up in a physical exam by a general practitioner, often when a young person is being checked out before going out for a sport. It is usually identified after adolescence, and there's some speculation that it may evolve gradually or it may simply be that young children, as a rule, don't get their hearts carefully checked.

We should note that there are plenty of perfectly benign heart murmurs that are not mitral valve prolapse. For example, women with slight anemia can have a typical benign murmur. If you're told by a doctor that you have a murmur, it may be one of these. Don't assume that it's mitral valve prolapse. A doctor may say, "Oh, you have a little murmur here, and maybe eventually we'll do an echocardiogram though managed care won't allow us to do that unless you have a higher-risk profile. But if you have any symptoms, we'll check it out further."

Sometimes I see patients who have already been told they have mitral valve prolapse. Often, when I see new patients with a bewildering array of symptoms which fit the general pattern, I ask them if they've ever been told they have mitral valve prolapse, and they say, "Yes, such and such a doctor mentioned that." Then I ask if anyone has ever told them this might have something to do with their symptoms. The answer is usually no. I see a lot of these patients because they have such a curious range of unusual symptoms which medical practitioners don't usually put together into the MVP profile. But these patients know very well that something is wrong with them.

On other occasions, I make the first diagnosis myself—and this is not just with young people. I'll do a physical exam for a new patient and hear the distinctive heart sounds—a faint murmur or the click the valve makes when it snaps open. I then may have an echocardiogram done and find the patient does have MVP. The fact is, there are a lot of people walking around with this who haven't been diagnosed because no one has listened to their hearts carefully enough or to their symptoms thoughtfully enough to put the picture together.

Very often I see patients who have been told they have hypochondriasis or "somatization disorder," which is another way of suggesting that they are translating their emotional anxieties into physical symptoms. In fact, it's really the other way around: they are having real physical symptoms that are causing them a lot of anxiety and worry because the symptoms are so diffuse and difficult to pin down and diagnose. Ironically, if you read the psychiatrists' diagnostic bible, the DSM-IV, the symptoms for somatization disorder really sound like the symptoms for mitral valve prolapse. It's clear then, how this confusion arises. Sometimes I even see people who are in psychotherapy and are trying to "talk through" the anxieties that are supposedly causing their symptoms, when they are actually suffering from a complex physical disorder.

When patients come to my office in a state of panic and confusion, either with or without the diagnosis of mitral valve prolapse, I can often ease their anxieties. When I tell them, "I see this all the time in mitral valve prolapse people," they are amazed and relieved. It's no longer "in their heads," no longer their isolated burden. They ask, "You mean all this stuff is connected?" And I assure them it is.

In fact, one of the most important strategies for coping with any disorder is cognitive therapy or cognitive reframing. If patients can intellectually understand and reposition the meaning of their symptoms, this can help them objectify their symptoms and get a little therapeutic distance from them. When we use universal, global statements like "Stress is making me feel crazy" or "I feel like I'm losing control," this tends to amplify symptoms. Better to say something specific and delimiting, like "There goes that reaction again. I know what that's about, it's just the syndrome acting up and I expect this to happen from time to time. It'll go away shortly as it always does." This is the beginning of learning to cope with MVP, so I usually spend some time with MVP patients to make sure they really understand the complex nature of their condition.

The Diagnostic Process

We currently have a high-tech system for evaluating conditions that cause heart murmurs called echocardiography. In the days before echocardiography, listening to the heart was quite an art.

Doctors would listen to it or "auscultate" it directly with the stethoscope. By evaluating heart sounds as to their differing locations in the chest and back and determining whether they were stronger here or weaker there, they would come up with a diagnosis of a particular kind of heart murmur. Now the diagnosis can be confirmed by taking an echocardiogram, which uses ultrasound to give a picture of the chambers of the heart.

For all of its benefits, echocardiography is not an exact and conclusive procedure. Reading an echocardiogram involves a certain degree of interpretation. The radiologist must look at a picture of an anatomical structure and make a somewhat subjective interpretation. It's not a quantitative finding like one's cholesterol level. There are people who have been through a succession of echocardiograms to try to find an explanation for their nervous symptoms; some doctors will read the pictures and find mitral valve prolapse and some will read the pictures differently and make a negative diagnosis. This is not always a hard and fast diagnosis, and in fact there is a whole spectrum of differing degrees of abnormality of the mitral valve. Some cases will be very clear-cut and others borderline or "subclinical." It's often not an either/or proposition.

People with mitral valve prolapse may experience troubling heart palpitations, skipped beats or irregular heartbeats that are sometimes real and quantifiable. There's a test device called the Holter monitor that patients can carry around for a day or a week that will record these symptoms. The device may reveal an impressive but usually harmless array of speed-ups and slow-downs and occasional benign skipped beats. These symptoms are aggravating but don't pose any danger. They're just part of the syndrome.

Tests for the underlying autonomic instability have long been part of the routine office physical exam. Sitting up or standing up from a lying position is a simple physical act that entails a complex series of adaptations by the autonomic nervous system. When the autonomic response is appropriate, blood vessels contract as we stand to maintain blood pressure. The heart rate speeds up slightly to compensate for the additional work needed to pump blood into the neck, shoulders and brain. If these mechanisms are flawed, we feel dizzy, "see stars" and may even faint. As a patient sits up or stands, a physician can thus note normal, exaggerated or even paradoxical blood pressure and heart rate responses to evaluate the autonomic reflexes.

A high-tech refinement of this traditional exam is the tilt-table test, recently popularized in a breakthrough study on the nature and treatment of chronic fatigue syndrome. In this test, patients are hooked up to an IV and placed on a tilt-table that can swivel them from lying flat to standing upright in seconds. Their heart rate and blood pressure responses to the position changes and infusions of catecholamine-mimicking drugs can be recorded. If severe autonomic dysfunction is observed, these people are often prescribed traditional heart drugs such as beta-blockers. My personal experience with administering such drugs to patients with sensitive autonomic responses is not so positive.

It should be noted that there are rare examples of more extreme and advanced cases of mitral valve prolapse that may require extra testing and more careful monitoring. The echocardiogram may reveal that there is some degree of backflow of blood through the weakened valve when the heart contracts. (The medical term for this is regurgitation.) When blood doesn't move properly through the heart, fluid can build up in the lungs. Since the veins aren't returning blood effectively to the heart, fluid can sometimes build up in the ankles as well. In very severe mitral valve disease there is sometimes enlargement of the left atrium, one of the heart's four chambers.

If someone has a pronounced case of mitral valve prolapse, is growing older and has increasing shortness of breath, we would want to monitor him or her more carefully. We would want to evaluate whether this might be true cardiac shortness of breath and not the more harmless hyperventilation syndrome that people with mitral valve prolapse tend to have. We might use a test called cardiac catheterization to see if they are really having some sort of serious valve failure, which is a rare consequence of a tiny minority of mitral valve prolapses. This test involves injecting dye into one chamber of the heart and measuring the speed of passage to the other chamber to get a very accurate measurement of the rate of flow of blood through the heart. A very pronounced valve failure, with backflow of blood in the heart, might suggest the option of valvular replacement. But these cases are very, very rare.

On other fronts, the French have been developing an interesting test for the condition called latent tetany, which is often associated with mitral valve prolapse. Tetany means an extended contraction or rigidity of the muscles, in this case of muscles involved in involuntary reflexes, such as the muscles that contract when someone taps your knee. It's latent because the muscles don't contract unless the reflex is induced. In people with mitral valve prolapse, the muscles take a little longer to relax after the reflex contraction is induced. In fact, people with mitral valve prolapse seem to have a high degree of neuromuscular irritability, more profound reflex responses and a more easily induced startle reaction to sudden noises. The French have developed instruments for measuring the speed of relaxation of the muscle after a reflex contraction. This is another marker for the general state of autonomic instability.

Interestingly, latent tetany is influenced by many factors, including calcium and magnesium levels, catecholamines and even the acid-base balance of the body. The new tests may be a way of measuring magnesium status at the cellular level. Blood magnesium levels vary across a range and may imperfectly reflect intracellular magnesium use where it counts. Some people may require higher levels of magnesium in their blood to have a more normal muscle tone.

HYBRID SYNDROMES: MVP AND OTHER CHRONIC AILMENTS

The mitral valve prolapse syndrome manifests itself through a rather bewildering constellation of symptoms. When someone has additional chronic health disorders, the combination can be even more distressing (and more difficult to diagnose). Let's look at how mitral valve prolapse can amplify or exaggerate symptoms of some other diseases or syndromes and complicate the diagnostic picture.

Chronic Fatigue Syndrome

Chronic fatigue syndrome (CFS) is to some extent a misnomer since it refers to a cluster of conditions which may have multiple causes. It leaves people feeling exhausted, debilitated, "tired all the time," but also sick in a way that resembles viral illness so the term chronic fatigue syndrome doesn't really do justice to the wide spectrum of symptoms that people experience.

A high percentage of people with chronic fatigue syndrome also have mitral valve prolapse. The reason for this is unclear. It may be that patients with mitral valve prolapse are in some way more "neurasthenic," to use a 19th century word. That is, they may be more vulnerable to debilitating illnesses. It may also be that since people with mitral valve prolapse are more susceptible to allergies, chemical sensitivities, and antibiotic-induced yeast infections, some of these conditions may render them more prone to CFS. Whatever the case, people who have both mitral valve prolapse and CFS often exhibit a bewildering and (for the doctor) challenging array of symptoms. These are largely autonomic in nature. They may experience rapid and unpredictable fluctuations of energy levels so that they feel exhausted at times when they want to be active and agitated, restless or hyper when they are trying to sleep or relax. It's as if they've lost control of their involuntary nervous system, which no longer responds in a normal way to the rhythms of daily life. They frequently feel wired, but tired.

Irritable Bowel Syndrome

Irritable bowel syndrome, another Mulligan's stew of possible disorders, can range from undiscovered parasite infestation to food allergies. But the more intrinsic type of irritable bowel syndrome seems closely linked to an autonomic disorder. Researchers are arriving at a new understanding of the "brain in the stomach," a "visceral brain" with an extended network of neurons and a highly active flow of neurotransmitter hormones that rivals the brain in the skull in its activity. One can well imagine how a disruption of this system can induce a wide array of gastrointestinal disorders. Moreover, since many people with mitral valve prolapse chronically use preventive courses of antibiotics when they see their dentists, this can set them up for yeast (candida) infections that can exaggerate intestinal problems. Symptoms may include bloating, constipation and/or diarrhea, independently or alternating with each other.

The hormonal flood of catecholamines that we call the "fight or flight" response can in some cases prompt defecation. The first reaction a soldier may have at the front, no matter how primed for combat he may be, is to lose control of his bowels as the guns begin to roar. This is a simple adaptive reflex to prepare animals for flight. After this initial reaction, digestion is halted, the wave of contractions that move food through the digestive tract (peristalsis) shuts down, and blood flow is diverted from the gut. As a result, initial diarrhea may be followed by constipation in unpredictable cycles.

Allergies and Food Sensitivities

Allergies and sensitivities can cause multiple shifting symptoms that often overlap with mitral valve prolapse symptoms. These can include digestive upset, but also fatigue, spaciness, and difficulty breathing. The allergic reaction causes the release of a compound called histamine, which constricts small breathing tubes in the lungs, choking off the flow of air. This can compound the feelings of breathlessness that are common among people with mitral valve prolapse. In the gut, allergic reactions can create a constant state of inflammation that can compound the symptoms of mitral valve prolapse.

Candida Infection

Those who have been given prophylactic or preventive antibiotics are especially prone to an overgrowth of yeast or candida infection in the gut. The symptoms of indigestion, bloating, diarrhea, constipation, fatigue or spaciness overlap with others caused by autonomic imbalance.

Multiple Chemical Sensitivity (MCS)

In the new field of environmental medicine we are identifying a type of patient we call a "universal reactor." This is a person who appears to be reacting with hypersensitivity to many environmental influences, including food additives, chemicals in the environment, dry cleaning chemicals, smells from plastic or vinyl or the detergent aisle in the grocery store. These stimuli can set off a cascade of distressing reactions. Conventional medicine views this as a delusional state and suggests that these people are phobic to foods or smells and suffer from depression or panic disorder. A more enlightened view is that these patients have suffered various environmental insults, such as living or working in an unventilated space with overwhelming paint or new carpet fumes, which have triggered their multiple sensitivity. People with mitral valve prolapse may have an underlying susceptibility to environmental stimuli that helps trigger this condition.

People with MCS are especially prone to amplification cycles of the nervous system which can set off a crescendo of worsening reactions leading to a generalized anxiety and loss of confidence in the safety of the environment. This is a challenging syndrome to deal with, but the multiple reactions can usually be reduced through allergy desensitization, proper nutritional support, detoxification and temporary shielding from environmental triggers.

"Sugar Disease"

The overconsumption of sugar and simple carbohydrates is perhaps the most common abuse of the body in America today. Our high-carbohydrate, sugar-laden diet leads ultimately to some form of sugar disease, from hypoglycemia to diabetes. Sugar and carbohydrate snacking take a tremendous toll on the body's metabolic machinery by triggering fatiguing surges of insulin and counter-regulatory stress hormones. Mitral valve prolapse can compound or exaggerate the symptoms of hypoglycemia, including spaciness, fatigue, mood changes, cravings, headaches, tremors, depression, hot flashes, palpitations, cold extremities, abdominal pain, panic attacks and violent mood and energy swings.

Fibromyalgia

This troubling but little-known ailment strikes women predominantly, developing typically when they are in their 30s or 40s, and is characterized by an achy body, muscle pain and sleep disturbances. It can lead to insomnia, irritable bowel syndrome and depression as can mitral valve prolapse, so both may contribute to chronic suffering. Fibromyalgia may be the result of some sort of nerve feedback loop that originates in the brain and feeds back pain symptoms to specific points in the body. In fact, there are 17 specific pairs of "trigger points" of pain that confirm the diagnosis.

Atypical Chest Pain Syndrome

This is one of the most perplexing medical entities that doctors and patients confront. When someone comes in and reports chest pain, physicians try to assign it to a category according to the possible cause—cardiac, pulmonary, gastrointestinal, musculoskeletal or psychiatric. Chest pain can result from heart disease, lung problems, trauma to the chest wall, inflammation of the rib cage, heartburn . . . and then there are possible psychiatric causes if all of the above can be ruled out. It's common, though, for people with mitral valve prolapse to have what we might call "phantom" chest pain that has no apparent physiological or even psychiatric cause. It appears to be a direct manifestation of the autonomic nervous system, not based in any disease process. However, it's nonetheless real pain. It resembles the way that amputees may experience pain in their "phantom limb"; even though their leg or arm has been amputated, they can still feel pain in it. Phantom chest pain is not caused by the mitral valve directly. Those who suffer from this are not "feeling their valve"; they are feeling a phantom expression of the autonomic nervous system in the chest.

A related phenomenon is hyperawareness of the heartbeat, which seems to grow louder and more insistent, raising anxiety. The sensation calls to mind Poe's classic horror story, "The Tell-Tale Heart." In the story, the murderer has cleverly dismembered his victim, scattered the body parts, and buried the heart under the floorboards of the house. But under interrogation by the police, he suddenly becomes aware of the faint and distant thumping of a heart, which grows inexorably louder. As his apprehension and anxiety grow and the police chat pleasantly, he screams out, "You're mocking me, I admit the deed!—tear up the planks!— here, here!—surely you all hear it!—it is the beating of his heart!" Plenty of moral, law-abiding citizens have experienced something similar for no apparent reason. And in fact, there is no physiological causation other than the general hypersensitivity of the autonomic system.

Hyperventilation Syndrome

Hyperventilation syndrome—breathing in increasingly rapid, shallow breaths—is a pervasive medical problem, and many people throughout the population suffer from this bad breathing habit. Shortness of breath and hyperventilation are also among the most common symptoms of mitral valve prolapse. People with this syndrome can get into a real state of panic with the sensation that they just can't draw a deep breath, can't get enough oxygen.

Menopause

Mitral valve prolapse tends to induce wild fluctuations in the levels of adrenal hormones, which can interact with the hormonal swings of menopause to exaggerate hot flashes, mood swings, hypoglycemia and the like. In fact, the hot flashes of menopause are cardinal signs of autonomic nervous system dysfunction.

Depression

Depression is pervasive in American society, with estimates that as many as 10 to 30 percent of Americans experience some form of intermittent depression. People with mitral valve prolapse make up a good part of this group and often experience a particular variety of depression that involves anxiety and a tendency toward phobic and obsessive thinking. Unlike many patients with depression, these people respond poorly or atypically to medication. They often report "impossible" drug reactions to their psychiatrists, such as having exaggerated sensitivity to very low doses of Prozac or traditional antidepressants. They seem to experience something like a "Princess and the Pea" syndrome, reminiscent of the fairy tale about the princess who lay on 7 mattresses and couldn't sleep a wink because of a single hard pea under the bottom mattress. You wouldn't think people could be sensitive to such small dosages of medications, but they are. They experience a combination of depression and anxiety marked by feelings of hopelessness, along with a disturbing physical reaction to medication that makes their care and treatment doubly challenging.

TURNING IT ALL AROUND: A CASE STUDY

Ann was a well-dressed, graceful lady who appeared in my office with a tragic air about her. The first thing she said to me was, "Dr. Hoffman, I hope you have plenty of time for me because everything is falling apart." Ann was 43, had been to multiple physicians and specialists and told me that her next stop was a psychiatric clinic if I couldn't help her. She told me she was plagued by a host of weird symptoms that she couldn't make any sense of and neither could all the doctors she'd seen. Ann said,

I'm losing my memory, my vision gets blurry, my hands and feet tingle —they don't feel like they're attached to my body. I'm sensitive to everything, foods, chemicals . . . I think I'm allergic to water. I can't eat anything—every time I eat I feel awful for hours afterward. I feel extremely weak and tired all the time but when I try to rest, I can't relax. My heart races, and I keep having a sensation like I can't catch my breath. I have difficulty falling asleep and sleeping through the night. I'm sensitive to noise—background noises just irritate me and loud noises make me jump. When I'm in the city and a siren goes by or somebody honks a horn my heart starts racing and I think I'm going to jump out of my skin.

I've been to a cardiologist, I've been to a gastroenterologist. I've been to a neurologist because I thought I had multiple sclerosis. I've been to an endocrinologist because I thought I had a thyroid problem. I've had all these tests for chronic fatigue syndrome and for Lyme disease, but they say I don't have them. I've taken antibiotics, but they didn't help. I'm on a healthy low-fat diet, and now I'm trying to fast and drink just fruit juice to clean out my system. I've tried everything.

I even went to a psychiatrist who said I have panic disorder. But Dr. Hoffman, I have nothing to be panicked about. I have a marvelous marriage, my husband says I don't have to work if I don't want to, I paint and I used to really enjoy it, but I can't paint now because the paint smells bother me. We have a wonderful summer house with my own studio in the back, but I can't go into it any more since we had some construction done. My kids are wonderful, one is going to Stanford, the other to Harvard—I couldn't ask for better.

I know it's not stress, because I don't really have much stress in my life. But I'm going crazy because I don't know what's happening to me. It's affecting my whole life—I'm afraid to go out any more because I'm thinking about this all the time and I'm afraid something is going to start my heart racing if I leave the house. One of the doctors told me I'm premenopausal, and some of my friends talk about the hot flashes and so on, but nothing like this.

Well, I listened to all this and noticed her hands, which were very broad, as broad as mine. In fact, a large hand span is a cardinal sign of mitral valve prolapse. So as I was doing a medical history with her, I asked if she'd ever been told she had a heart murmur. Sure enough, the cardiologist had told her she had an "innocent" murmur. We did the echocardiogram, and it showed she clearly had mitral valve prolapse. This was just the beginning with Ann because I really had to take some time to begin to convince her that she was not going crazy, that we could help her and that there was a logical explanation for all her symptoms.

In fact, it took Ann several visits to really come to understand her condition and accept it. Meanwhile, we developed the diet, nutritional supplements and exercise program that ultimately relieved the meltdown of her autonomic nervous system (see pages 30–42). Because she had had no cognitive framework through which to understand her symptoms, she really had been starting to feel crazy and she had been developing an amplified phobic response to her paints, her summer house and to going out. Ann was probably inherently susceptible to chemicals and had some food allergies, so MVP wasn't necessarily the whole picture, but it was a big part. Her low-fat high-carbohydrate diet was alternately boosting and crashing her blood sugar levels, calling up an adrenaline rush every time they bottomed out. The juice fast only made this worse. This and the antibiotics also promoted a chronic yeast infection. In the end, Ann's diet, chemical sensitivities, magnesium deficiency and the hormonal shifts of menopause were all combining with the autonomic instability of mitral valve prolapse to send her around the bend. We had to take her by the hand and lead her back, but after a year she is painting again, perfectly happy, with a new set of tools to manage her condition. For Ann, understanding was the key.

CONVENTIONAL MEDICAL TREATMENT

The medical perspectives on mitral valve prolapse fall into three main camps. The conventional medical establishment says "This is a benign anatomical variation of no real consequence. If you're having weird symptoms you're probably transforming your mental anxiety into physical symptoms when it's all in your head. But by the way, you need to take antibiotics every time you have a dental procedure." The enlightened medical establishment would go farther to say that "Yes, this is a real syndrome, and we understand you really are suffering. You can learn to recognize the symptoms, learn to live with them and help them to some extent with medications and exercise." Holistic physicians like me go even further. I recommend aggressive treatment on several fronts—behavioral, nutritional and physical. I like my patients to have a really good understanding of what is going on so they're not left feeling like "cardiac cripples."

DIAGNOSIS AND FOLLOW-UP

One of the worst results of making the diagnosis of mitral valve prolapse is that people become very apprehensive about their hearts since they don't completely understand the syndrome. They will often tend to avoid exercise because they are afraid of some kind of reaction from their "weak heart" when actually proper exercise is what they really need.

Accordingly, many doctors tend not to want to confuse patients with information that they don't think will be clearly understood. In the belief that the majority of their patients are medically illiterate or just won't be able to understand, they sometimes decide to withhold the diagnosis of mitral valve prolapse, particularly if they believe the patient has hypochondriacal or "somatization" tendencies. This may be well-meaning, since heart murmur does spell fear to many people and it does take time to explain the ins and outs of mitral valve prolapse. But ultimately it's not to the patient's benefit to conceal this.

The fact is, mitral valve prolapse does not affect longevity or long-range health, though there is a very small percentage of people who have this in a very pronounced form who go on to develop some complications. The issue of treatment is controversial even within the medical mainstream—some say there's no need for any treatment and others say that a diagnosis should be followed up with further tests and tracking. But the condition is so rarely associated with any serious cardiac problems that this is mostly unnecessary. We don't normally need to keep going back for tests as we do with blood pressure or cholesterol levels.

If someone showed a fairly pronounced condition on the echocardiogram, I'd want to track this with another picture every few years, but otherwise this really isn't necessary. Repeated follow-ups can themselves become a nerve-wracking process for the patient. Once mitral valve prolapse is diagnosed, it's just there. If someone began to develop new symptoms, like breathlessness when climbing stairs, that might indicate that the valve problem is advancing. The problem is, it's not necessarily helpful to ask MVP patients to take note of whether they're breathless climbing stairs because they tend to have a greater likelihood of feeling breathless and to hyperventilate anyway.

MEDICATION

We live in a drug-happy culture with a drug-happy medical system, so the doctors who do acknowledge MVP are liable to prescribe all kinds of medications to help with symptoms. They will sometimes prescribe anti-anxiety medications such as Buspar, Klonopin, Xanax or Ativan (replacing Valium, the old stand-by). The problem is, all of these have side effects plus an addictive potential. When they are discontinued they produce "rebound" anxiety and they don't really address the underlying condition as effectively as the holistic treatments I will describe later.

The use of beta-blockers is popular with some physicians, who cite their success in combating stage fright or speaker's phobia. This is a class of drugs typically prescribed to reduce blood pressure and offered to MVP patients with the intent to "calm them down." Common beta-blockers include Inderal and Tenormin. These powerful drugs commonly cause significant side effects including lethargy, low blood pressure, elevated cholesterol and impotence. Worse, beta-blockers may actually have the reverse effect of what's intended and stimulate the autonomic nervous system into a condition of rebound hypersensitivity, thus mimicking the symptoms of MVP.

SIDE EFFECTS OF BETA BLOCKERS

- Depression
- Headaches
- Vertigo and dizziness
- Insomnia
- Shortness of breath
- Cold hands and feet
- Gastrointestinal upset
- Dry mouth
- Constipation

"PREVENTIVE" ANTIBIOTIC TREATMENT

One treatment that's universally pressed on people with mitral valve prolapse is preventive or prophylactic antibiotic treatment. The typical setting is the dentist's office. You go to see a new dentist and you conscientiously check off the box for heart murmur on the questionnaire that's handed you. The dentist then refuses to do any work on your teeth unless you take a course of antibiotics and will repeat this every time you have a dental procedure. You'll run into the same thing with some kinds of medical tests such as a sigmoidoscopy which looks for intestinal polyps and even minor surgeries such as suturing a cut in a doctor's office.

Why the concern? Some heart murmurs and valve implants are associated with some increased risk if endocarditis, a bacterial infection of the heart valves. We all normally carry bacteria in our mouths, and it's thought that the slightly stickier surfaces of a prolapsed mitral valve can trap bacteria that may be released into the bloodstream as teeth are cleaned or fillings drilled. (The fact is, even when you brush your teeth you generally cause some bacteria to enter the bloodstream.) Endocarditis is one of the worst kinds of infection you can have. It's a devastating disease that before the antibiotic era usually led to death, and even now it normally requires a six-week course of very powerful intravenous antibiotics.

The fact is that there is a very, very slight statistical increase of rates of endocarditis in people with mitral valve prolapse. It's barely statistically significant, something like four cases per one million dental procedures, but it's enough to scare the whole medical and legal system into decreeing that everyone with the condition needs prophylactic antibiotics in a variety of situations. So MVP patients tend to get bombarded with antibiotics. As a result, they often have some of the predictable side effects including the disruption of the intestinal flora known as candida infection. Ultimately the widespread antibiotic overuse will aid the spread of antibiotic-resistant bacteria.

Now, in someone who has a serious heart murmur or a heart valve replacement, there is some justification for the propohylactic antibiotic treatment. But in my opinion, this is not required for most people with mitral valve prolapse. It should be necessary in only the most pronounced cases, where there is a clearly diagnosed backflow of blood through the heart. My position is controversial. Most dentists who find out that you have any kind of heart murmur won't touch you unless you're on antibiotics. But I think we all need to be much more concerned about the overuse of antibiotics, which is causing a serious increase in the number of diseases with multiple resistances to all but the most powerful and expensive new drugs. Further, antibiotic overuse can promote candida (yeast) infections, which are especially troublesome for mitral valve prolapse patients because they may be more immunologically susceptible.

Recent studies confirm that antibiotic treatment for MVP patients is neither cost-effective nor useful. One suggests that the risk of endocarditis is lowered from 4 in one million to 1.8 in one million, which is about equivalent to the risk of a fatal penicillin reaction to the antibiotic. The studies agree that antibiotic treatment should be limited to those with pronounced murmurs.

Dental Anesthesia

Beyond the antibiotic issue, MVP patients run additional risks when they visit their dentists and have dental work done that requires a shot of local anesthetic such as Novocaine or lidocaine. These anesthetics are often laced with the catecholamine called epinephrine. This is added because it makes the blood vessels constrict and keeps the anesthesia localized in the immediate area of the injection so it doesn't get carried off by the bloodstream. That little bit of epinephrine in the injection can cause havoc in MVP patients who are hypersensitive to it. They may have an intolerance reaction with strong autonomic symptoms during and after the dental visit. They will think they're allergic to the anesthetic when they're actually responding to the epinephrine. Worse, this may increase their fear of dental work to the point of phobia. If you have mitral valve prolapse, consider asking your dentist for local anesthesia without the epinephrine.

ASTHMA TREATMENT

If you have mitral valve prolapse you are already prone to hyperventilation and shortness of breath. If you develop a bad bronchitis, you may experience an asthmatic reaction along with it, with the sensation that you can't catch your breath. You go to the emergency room where you get the standard treatment for an asthma attack—a shot of epinephrine. This opens up the breathing, but it's precisely the medication that will send you into a state of autonomic hypersensitivity. Now you're scared, anxious and starting to hyperventilate and still can't breathe. Next you are given intravenous drugs which are synthetic versions of caffeine, preventing the reabsorption of the catecholamines that are now washing through your system. They do open up your lungs, but by now you are feeling terrible, devastated by the medications. You are sent home with the assurance that your asthma attack has been treated and you'll be fine. You may be given an inhaler to take home which can start you on a real roller coaster. You may have chest pressure which you interpret as shortness of breath, you start to hyperventilate again and use the inhaler which will make the chest symptoms even worse.

Some people race into their doctor's office or emergency room repeatedly with symptoms like this and are given massive doses of the very drugs that will throw their autonomic nervous system into chaos. What I do with such people is give them a peak flow meter to take home. This is a little handheld device that measures lung capacity so you can test yourself and demonstrate to yourself that your airways are clear despite the chest sensations. It's a good reality check. Most people can use this to convince themselves that the medications are less necessary. They can practice some of the antihyperventilation techniques discussed on page 35, and watch the syndrome unravel.

ALTERNATIVE MEDICAL TREATMENTS

The good news is that there is a whole array of natural therapies for people with mitral valve prolapse which can help alleviate the multiple symptoms. They range from behavioral therapies to diet modifications and nutritional supplements. Many of the therapies help by affecting the core phenomenon of mitral valve prolapse, which is instability of the autonomic nervous system.

COGNITIVE THERAPY

This is the basic ground for the holistic approach to mitral valve prolapse. It's important for everyone with MVP to seek out a sympathetic or holistic physician who can clearly explain the variety of possible symptoms, confirm that they are not imaginings or hypochondriasis and provide a program of treatment. If you understand clearly what is happening, you can learn ways to block the feedback loops that can lead to panic attacks or hyperventilation and break the cycle. By performing a reality check, you can learn to break the conditioned response you have acquired to your own physical symptoms.

The human brain has a tremendous evolutionary advantage. We can think of danger as an abstraction, as a future possibility. Animals can't do this—for them danger is a clear and present reality or else it's absent. Animals don't imagine danger, they sense it. Humans, however, have a massive forebrain which permits abstract thought and imagination. This has tremendous survival advantages. It means we can anticipate; we can plan to avoid danger. But we can be victims of this same adaptation. We can experience the physiological reaction to danger when the danger is merely imagined and not present, and this response can run away with us. We are conditioned in so many ways in the modern world to be motivated by fear, and rightly so, because it's a dangerous world. If we step off the curb in front of traffic we can be killed or maimed; if we snarl at a boss or a client we can lose our means of livelihood. But the problem is that we can experience fear as an abstraction in response to our thoughts when there is no clear and present danger or no likely future danger. This response is deeply imprinted in our physiology and can be amplified by our ability to remember, think and visualize.

Now, our capability for abstract thought and visualization can also be a powerful tool for good. We can envision goals and construct long-range plans to achieve them. We can also affect our physiology through visualization—by envisioning scenes of beauty, relaxation, serenity—or through different forms of prayer or meditation. Even the most anxious person has experiences of peace, comfort, or spiritual surrender which can be remembered and evoked, so it's entirely possible to alter one's physiology to induce calm even when circumstances are difficult.

Unfortunately, most people tend to exercise the mental muscle that evokes the fear reaction rather than the one that evokes the relaxation response. The good news is, you can train this mental muscle and make it work for you.

Let's look at how negative thought amplification works and how to break the cycle. You feel a little sick and dizzy after supper and you say, "I feel sick tonight, I probably won't be able to go to work tomorrow, my boss will think I'm goofing off if I don't go to work and even if I do, I won't be very effective. I probably won't be very good at the meeting with our client, there's a good chance we'll lose the account and if I make us lose the account, I can't ask for the raise like I was planning. I won't be able to keep up with my bills, I might lose the house, then I'd probably lose my job, my home, I'll be out on the streets, and this is to be expected because I've always been a failure at everything!" Now you're really sick with worry and you think you're going to have trouble getting to sleep, which means you won't get enough rest, which means you probably really will be sick tomorrow, etc. Now your heart is pounding and you feel even more dizzy and have to lie down. This is called free-floating anxiety. What can you do about it? Here are some tools of cognitive therapy you might use:

- If you know you're prone to free-floating anxiety, remind yourself that you're engaging in nonproductive thinking. Think STOP, I don't have to take any of this seriously, this kind of thinking is just a bad habit I have.
- Expand the range of possibilities. When you're worrying like this you're probably limiting yourself to thinking only about the *bad* possibilities. Perform a reality check. Ask yourself, "If I'm sick tomorrow, what's the worst thing that will happen, what's the best, what's in between?" Maybe the meeting will be postponed, and you'll stay home and come up with a new idea that will really impress the client and your boss. Maybe the meeting will have to be postponed for reasons that have nothing to do with you. Mark Twain was talking about free-floating anxiety when he said, "I've been through a lot of terrible situations in my life. And some of them actually happened."
- Bring yourself back to the present moment, what is happening right now. If you're thinking, "I won't have the money to pay the rent, I'm going to be evicted, I'll lose my job, I'll be homeless," ask yourself, "*Right now*, do I have food to eat? Do I have some clothes to wear? Do I have a roof over my head?"
- Schedule your time for worrying. Pick a couple of times a day, say at 11:30 a.m. and again at 4 p.m. When the time comes, stop whatever you're doing, take 15 minutes or half an hour and just worry. Let yourself think about all the scary, dangerous, terrible things that might happen. Concentrate on all your worries and really do it. Most people find that after about five minutes they just can't do it any more—they become conscious of the transient and insubstantial nature of most anxious thoughts.

The Guatemalans do this with little figures they call worry dolls. They tell each doll a worry, put it in a basket, and then walk away. Later they go back and consult the worry dolls after they've worked it all out.

These techniques don't require that you go into therapy, figure out why you're so anxious, what your parents did to you or whether you have a neurosis. These are not analytical tools—they are result oriented.

MEDITATION AND RELAXATION TECHNIQUES

Studies have shown that meditation and relaxation techniques are effective in a whole array of serious chronic illnesses and have measurable physiological effects. They can relieve stress, help alleviate chronic pain and even lower blood pressure. They are especially helpful for people with mitral valve prolapse, whose symptoms are worsened by stress.

You don't need a guru, you don't have to learn to sit in the lotus position and you don't have to join a cult to benefit from these practices. You can get started just by sitting quietly in an upright position with eyes open or closed and mentally counting from one to three or four as you slowly breathe in, and then counting backward as you slowly breathe out. Don't try to clear your mind of thoughts and feelings, but allow them to arise normally. Simply observe them with detachment as they appear in your consciousness while continuing to count and be aware of your slow, easy, regular breathing. Do this for 10 to 15 minutes once or twice a day and you're on your way to establishing a neurophysiological "oasis" that will have long-lasting beneficial effects.

Some people like to use a mantra, which can be a meaningless sound, or a word or phrase from one of the world's religions or wisdom traditions. Again, you repeat this sound or word mentally while remaining aware of your slow, regular breathing, allowing thoughts to rise freely into consciousness, simply observing them with detachment and returning to the mantra whenever your mind wanders.

There are a number of books that can help you with meditation and relaxation techniques, and there are centers at some hospitals and clinics that offer courses of instruction. Dr. Herbert Benson, founder of the Mind-Body Institute at Harvard Medical School, has written a useful book on these techniques called *The Relaxation Response*. Many people find they benefit from taking yoga classes, which combine peaceful relaxation with physical stretching.

Biofeedback
Biofeedback is a high-tech relaxation practice and it can be quite effective. A biofeedback therapist will select a physical marker, such as the tension of a facial muscle, hand temperature, or even

brain wave pattern, and hook up an electronic device to monitor this numerically so that the patient can observe it and try to move the numbers in a certain direction—toward a more relaxed muscle, warmed hand temperature—while watching the indicator. With some practice, the patient can learn to influence these markers of autonomic nervous tension even without the device.

EXERCISE

Mitral valve prolapse is not at all the sort of heart condition that should make anyone apprehensive about engaging in exercise. In fact, exercise is one of the best therapies we have for deconditioning learned sensitivities and relieving neurological symptoms. Studies have shown that people who engage in regular aerobic exercise report a decline in symptoms of chest pain, fatigue, dizziness, mood swings and panic attacks.

People with mitral valve prolapse are typically subject to fluctuating changes in heart rate, which speeds up and slows down erratically and not in response to normal challenges. Through periods of aerobic exercise alternating with rest, they can bring the heart rate up gradually, sustain it and gradually bring it back down. This will begin to establish more normal autonomic rhythms and will also strengthen the heart. Exercise also establishes a more normal balance of oxygen and carbon dioxide in the blood, which helps relieve symptoms of hyperventilation and shortness of breath. Regular exercise also seems to have a positive psychological effect, reducing or eliminating the reaction to situations and stresses that usually provoke symptoms.

A word of warning, though: exercise is a two-edged sword for those with mitral valve prolapse. Since exercise is inherently a catecholamine-releasing activity, overexertion can actually increase the symptoms of mitral valve prolapse. Exercise also causes a build-up of excess lactic acid that can provoke hyperventilation. In today's health clubs there are many people who fling themselves into aerobic shock, going from sedentary jobs to activities that challenge their performance limits. Aerobic exercise is extremely valuable for the MVP patient but should be undertaken in a paced, gradual way, moving toward stepped milestones. It can be helpful to ask your doctor for some specific heart rate targets and work with a trainer who understands this. The key is to avoid exceeding your physiological capacity and thereby setting off the kind of autonomic nervous reaction you're trying to avoid. An excellent way to start getting the benefits of exercise is to simply walk. You can gradually increase the pace and the length of your walks and then try some more aerobic exercise such as short periods of jogging or bicycling.

Try to standardize exercise conditions. It actually may be better to exercise on a treadmill or with a Nordic Track than to get into jogging in all kinds of weather. Embarking on a jog through hilly country on a windy winter day can place a huge load on your system. The cold can cause you to run faster than normal, unusual traffic can startle you to run faster than normal, or demand extra alertness, so that you turn beneficial exercise into stressful exercise without realizing it. If you're not autonomically resilient it's better to exercise under very controllable conditions where you can regulate the speed or slant of a treadmill and condition yourself gradually in small increments.

HYPERVENTILATION TREATMENT

When you hyperventilate you feel short of breath and ironically, the more you hyperventilate, the more short of breath you become. If you are hyperventilating, you feel that you must be short of oxygen, and logically you want to breathe more, so you start to pant. What happens? You increase your production of stress hormones and you also blow off carbon dioxide at an increased rate. When you blow off carbon dioxide, you develop an increased alkalinity of the blood (called alkalosis), which creates weird symptoms such as tingling and numbness of the fingers. And it makes you crave oxygen even more.

Hyperventilation also promotes magnesium deficiency since magnesium is an alkaline mineral that is excreted to compensate for the excess alkalinity in the blood. (This is just one of the ways that stress depletes magnesium.) Some people with mitral valve prolapse have a condition called "Ondine's curse" in which they are constantly aware of their breathing—an extreme form of hyperventilation. It turns out these people have lower magnesium levels, so giving them magnesium sometimes relieves their symptoms.

The first line of treatment, however, is behavioral. Paradoxically, the way to break the hyperventilation cycle is to build up more carbon dioxide in the bloodstream. You can do this in a few minutes by breathing into a paper bag. Another way is to consciously breathe with a slow outbreathing cycle: give yourself time to let your lungs empty after each inbreath.

Hyperventilators tend to breathe too quickly, up to 15 or 20 times per minute, even when they are not having a full-fledged attack. A normal resting respiration rate is probably 8 to 12 breaths per minute. This means that a complete cycle of inhalation and exhalation should last five to eight seconds. The meditation practice of counting while inhaling and exhaling is an excellent way of establishing a normal breathing rate.

One thing people with mitral valve prolapse can do is follow a singing teacher's advice and breathe from the diaphragm, the gut, and not from the chest. There are nerve receptors called proprioceptors in the chest, so if you breathe from your chest you can actually initiate the production of catecholamines. When I ask my patients to take a deep breath, I usually find they are breathing wrong, that is, from the chest. Breathing from the abdomen does not stimulate these receptors and in fact tends to trigger the relaxation response, No matter what you are feeling, you can mechanically make yourself relax just by breathing properly.

To make sure you are doing this, lie on your back, put one hand on your chest and the other on your stomach, and breathe so that you are moving the hand on your stomach and not the one on your chest. You can accentuate the effect by counting slowly as you breathe in, feeling the pause between breaths and counting slowly as you breathe out.

Swimming is an excellent exercise for breath control. To breathe properly while swimming, you turn your head out of the water to quickly gulp a new supply of air, and then s-l-o-w-l-y exhale with your head face down in the water as you take the next stroke or two.

Gentle stretching exercises such as yoga training, which involves breath control, can be extremely valuable as well. In Hindu tradition and in yoga practice the breath is the gateway to mind control. There are various types of yogic breathing exercises, some simple and some elaborate, which are designed to produce a meditative state.

NATURAL TREATMENT FOR RESPIRATORY PROBLEMS

Though most shortness of breath is caused by hyperventilation, people with mitral valve prolapse tend to be more allergic and reactive and sometimes have real asthmatic reactions. For this problem, they need to avoid pollutants that can set off the allergic asthmatic reaction—from paint and exhaust fumes, animal dander and feathers to cigarette smoke, perfume, cleaning fluids, dust and mold. There is mounting evidence that the very drugs used to treat asthma can worsen the condition over long use. Physical training in relaxed abdominal breathing, yogic breathing techniques and an exercise like swimming, with its requirement for controlled breathing, can help people cope with limited breathing capacity. Nutrients, especially the antioxidants—vitamins C, E and A, along with mixed carotenoids, zinc and selenium—can help put out the fire and reduce the inflammatory condition of asthma. Magnesium can act as a natural bronchodilator, relaxing the smooth muscle that lines the tiny tubules that bring air to the lungs so that it doesn't go into spasm. Higher intakes of Omega-3 oils also appear to help respiratory problems.

Acupuncture, the ancient Chinese healing art, is also helpful in mitigating the symptoms of asthma. In China, departments of pulmonary medicine, while adopting modern techniques of pharmacological management, always have skilled acupuncturists on staff.

DIET MODIFICATION

It's interesting that mitral valve prolapse is experienced more by young, slender women. Usually physically sensitive people, they tend to be especially attuned to health issues. Many of them are conscientious about having a good diet, and lately this has come to be synonymous with a low-fat diet. They carefully examine the nutrition panel on every product in the supermarket or health food store and steer toward the no-fat cookies and muffins, the lowfat frozen dinners and so on. Low fat content has become the hallmark of dietary virtue.

As a result, these women tend to eat a diet that is skewed toward carbohydrates and away from protein, which usually has some fat content. The high-carbohydrate diets make them especially susceptible to swings in blood sugar, caused by the breakdown of starches and even "natural" sugars into glucose, the culprit molecule. Even sugar derived from natural fruits can cause upward swings in blood sugar. There is a roller-coaster effect as each upward swing is followed by a crash, a period of extremely low blood sugar.

This results in a powerful internal stress. We're used to thinking of stress as external, but the body responds to low blood sugar in exactly the same way as it does to a perception of external danger: by releasing catecholamines. The autonomic response and the feeling are identical. The key is to avoid inflicting dietary stress on yourself and undo your body's call for catecholamines. They are there for a reason—to prevent fainting or seizure or cardiac arrest. They do their job, but at a price.

A high-carbohydrate, high-sugar diet promotes what I call "sugar disease," which ranges in severity across a whole spectrum from hypoglycemia to incipient diabetes. These are all conditions of blood sugar imbalance caused by the release of massive amounts of sugar into the bloodstream, which calls on the body to overproduce insulin and subsequently, catecholamines. The typical symptoms of spaciness, sudden fatigue and mood swings are amplified by mitral valve prolapse.

The first step in adjusting your diet should be to go off sugar completely or as much as possible. This means avoiding low-fat and no-fat cookies and muffins, which are high-carbohydrate, high-sugar items, as well as foods made with honey, maple syrup, corn syrup or molasses and fruit juice and soda, which normally contain 100–200 calories per serving from sugar.

Next, reduce the amount of low-fat high-carbohydrate foods in your diet and start emphasizing lean protein and complex carbohydrates like tofu and legumes. These provide the body with slowly released and steady levels of blood sugar in a protein- and fiber-rich matrix. Adding protein to the diet, whether as milk, meat, cheese or even eggs, tends to level out the swings in blood sugar; it serves as a kind of anchor. Beans and tofu are good sources of low-fat vegetable protein.

You can also even out the peaks and valleys in blood sugar levels by eating more frequently in smaller amounts. A solid breakfast is especially important since it sets up the "glycemic tone" of the day. Eating protein with breakfast will level out blood sugar from the beginning, so that later meals and snacks will perturb it less. By contrast, a muffin or piece of toast will boost the blood sugar immediately and set up a roller-coaster pattern for the day. Consider "nonbreakfast" meals to start the day, such as a bowl of lentil soup. Kasha, or buckwheat groats, is a good high-

---

GOOD LOW-CARBOHYDRATE SNACKS

Peanut or other nut butters on a rice cake
Hummus (a chickpea and sesame seed paste) on a rice cake
A hard-boiled egg instead of an apple
Low-fat cheese on a whole-grain cracker
Sardines or smoked salmon
Turkey slices
Yogurt dip with vegetables

---

protein alternative to sugar-laden high-carb cereals. Continue with a midmorning snack, lunch, a midafternoon snack, a light dinner and a bedtime snack. The snacks should not be sugar-laden or fruit-juice sweetened pastry or muffins; the lunch should not be high-carb pasta. Try to get a little protein into each of the meals and into the snacks.

Some fats can help control blood sugar swings. Omega-3 oils such as those found in flaxseed oil and cold water fish such as salmon, trout, tuna or the wild game our ancestors ate help level out blood sugar. Monounsaturated fats found in olive and canola oils also help adjust blood sugar. Of course, all fats should be eaten in moderation.

Avoid caffeine, drink 6 to 8 glasses of water a day and allow yourself moderate salt intake. Many people with mitral valve prolapse have hypotension; they have trouble sustaining sufficient blood pressure, which can result in a spacey, dizzy feeling. Moderate salt in the diet can help with this and with maintaining fluid volume in the blood. Don't go out of your way to avoid salty foods.

Finally, opt for magnesium-rich foods. These include vegetables and to some extent fruits, but keep fruits to about one or two per day. Nuts are also rich in magnesium.

The Glycemic Index for Foods

Researchers have established a measure of how quickly foods raise blood sugar levels. This measure is called the glycemic index and is based on the blood-glucose level caused by the food in comparison with pure glucose. The glycemic index (GI) is based on the concept that pure glucose has a 100 percent response—it is the ultimate, instantly usable sugar. High GIs create a peak in blood sugar levels which arouses a massive release of insulin to absorb them followed by a crash in blood sugar levels and a massive release of catecholamines. People with MVP should avoid foods with high GIs and seek out foods with low GIs.

Many foods we always thought were "good" carbohydrates may not be good for people with mitral valve prolapse. The form of a food has a great impact on the way it changes blood-sugar levels: flour in the form of spaghetti has a much lower glycemic index than flour in the form of bread. Adding butter or oil to potatoes or carrots will also lower their glycemic index, and whole milk is better than skim milk as far as the GI is concerned. A cardinal rule: eat as if the flour mill had never been invented. The milling process makes the starch inside grains more susceptible to digestion and rapid absorption of its sugar content and actually raises the glycemic index of a grain.

HIGH GLYCEMIC INDEX FOODS (Minimize)

Potatoes, especially instant mashed
Carrots
Corn flakes and processed cereals
Breads and muffins, both white and whole wheat
White rice
Fruit juices
Raisins and other dried fruit
Bananas
Milk and yoghurt, especially fat-free
Pastries and sweets

LOW GLYCEMIC INDEX FOODS (Emphasize)

Nuts
Legumes
Unmilled whole grains: brown rice, barley, bulgur, rolled oats, amaranth, quinoa
Eggs
Fish, poultry, lean meats
Most vegetables

Hydration Therapy

This is a fancy name for making sure that you get enough water and liquids to drink. Fluid is needed to maintain blood pressure, and the carotid arteries in the neck are lined with sensors called baroreceptors which sense the relative fullness or emptiness of the arteries. People with mitral valve prolapse may have more sensitive baroreceptors, so with insufficient fluid in their systems they will suffer from symptoms of weakness, wooziness, lightheadedness. The baroreceptors set off tumult in the autonomic nervous system. One way to avert this is to be conscientious about drinking water, at least 6 to 8 glasses per day.

NUTRITIONAL THERAPY

There are several key nutrients that can affect the underlying causes of mitral valve prolapse symptoms.

Magnesium is probably the most significant of these. Magnesium deficiencies are associated with migraine headaches and are common in people with epilepsy and mitral valve prolapse. Magnesium plays an important role in restoring cellular metabolism, replenishing depleted energy reserves, and acts as a catalyst for many of the body's energy reactions. As we've noted, magnesium seems to affect everything from breathing patterns to reflex muscle tension.
Oral dosage: Magnesium oxide or magnesium citrate, 150 to 200 mg 2 to 3 times daily. If diarrhea occurs, cut back dosage.

L-carnitine is an amino acid that acts as a shuttle for fat that is required for cellular matabolism. It can be used as a "cellular energizer" and also acts to strengthen the heart.
Dosage: 500–1,000 mg 2 to 3 times daily.
Acetyl-l-carnitine as an alternative, is a related nutrient that may be more bioavailable.
Dosage: 120 mg 3 times daily. Both should be taken between meals, since amino acids are best absorbed on an empty stomach.

Co-enzyme Q10 appears to improve disturbed bioenergetic function at the molecular level. It is an essential co-enzyme for energy production within the mitochondria, which are the "powerhouses" of cells, and is specifically helpful for patients suffering from a weakening of the heart. Co-enzyme Q-10 enhances pumping action of the heart, output of blood, speed of heart muscle contraction and general cardiac efficiency. It may also prove helpful for patients suffering from profound fatigue.
Dosage: 60 to 120 mg/day.

Several of the **B vitamins** can help with symptoms of mitral valve prolapse. Among other things, they can reduce high levels of lactic acid in the blood that are associated with anxiety and panic attack. (Experiments with volunteers have shown that infusing lactic acid into the blood can directly induce the panic response.) Alcohol, caffeine and sugar all contribute to higher lactic acid levels, and the B vitamins niacin and thiamin can help reduce them.
Dosage: Vitamin B_1 (thiamine) 100 mg/day; **Vitamin B_3** (niacin) 50 mg/day.
Vitamin B_6 (pyridoxine) can favor the production in the brain of higher levels of the relaxing and sedating neurotransmitter, serotonin. Prozac and Prozac-like drugs are prescribed to achieve the same effect.

Dosage: 50 mg/day.

Inositol is another B vitamin that acts as a calming agent.
Dosage: 3 to 6 grams/day.

HERBAL RELAXANTS

Kava *(Piper methysticum)* belongs to the pepper family and is used throughout the Pacific islands, often in the form of an intoxicating drink called kava-kava, which appears to induce a relaxed sociable state with lessened fatigue and anxiety, followed by a deep restful sleep with no hangover. Kava has been shown in therapeutic doses to be useful in dampening the symptoms of anxiety without the risk of dampening alertness or addiction. Double-blind studies have determined that kava-kava can be as effective as Valium-type drugs in reducing anxiety, yet does not combine adversely with alcohol. Its active components, the kava lactones, have a calming and anticonvulsive effect, and relax not only skeletal muscles but also the smooth muscle of the internal organs like the heart, the intestinal wall and the blood vessels, which are controlled by the autonomic nervous system.
Dosage: 100 to 200 mg of the standardized preparation of kava lactones per day.

Valerian *(Valeriana officinalis),* from the Western tradition of herbal healing, has a root that acts as an effective calmative agent and antispasmodic. It calms the central nervous system, relaxes smooth muscle tissue and is effective for insomnia with no morning aftereffects. Valerian should be used on an occasional basis or for acute conditions. A small percentage of people can develop atypical reactions to valerian, such as stimulation rather than relaxation.
Dosage: The effective dose can vary widely. Valerian is commonly available in capsule or tincture form. For acute conditions, ½ tsp. to 2 tsp. tincture of valerian up to every two hours.

Hops *(Humulus lupulus)* can also be helpful in calming nervous excitement and treating hysteria and insomnia. Hops should not be used in cases of depression.
Dosage: 1 cup of tea 3 times a day, or ¼ to ½ tsp. tincture 3 times a day or as needed.

Oil of **lavender,** an essential aromatic oil obtained from lavender plants, has a sedating effect on the central nervous system when inhaled. It may be especially helpful for sudden stress or hyperventilation. Sprinkle 1 or 2 drops of lavender oil on a cotton ball or tissue and inhale slowly and deeply. Do not take internally.

SUPPORT FOR ANTIBIOTIC THERAPY AND CANDIDA INFECTION

People with mitral valve prolapse may have been given unnecessary doses of preventive antibiotics, which can disturb the ecology of the body, especially the intestinal tract. If not properly managed, antibiotic treatment can induce vaginitis, gastrointestinal problems and secondary infections with candida yeast. Patients with these problems need to take measures to restore the balance of intestinal flora. Two dietary supplements can be especially useful.

Acidophilus. This is a natural culture of beneficial bacteria that can be used to help maintain the proper "ecological balance" in the digestive tract. Many brands of yogurt have active acidopohilus cultures, so one way to keep up the balance is to eat a cup of this type of yogurt (unsweetened) every day. Those who don't like yogurt or who may be allergic to milk products can take acidophilus in the form of a powder or capsules. *Dosage:* ¼ to ½ tsp. powder 3 times daily or 2 capsules 3 times daily.

Fructose oligosaccharides (FOS). This is a good food source for beneficial bacteria which does not fuel the growth of candida. *Dosage:* ½ tsp. 3 times daily.

ALLERGY TESTING AND TREATMENT

Symptoms of food allergies, intolerances and sensitivities can be amplified and worsened by mitral valve prolapse. These include spaciness, inability to concentrate, digestive upset and fatigue. Without realizing it, many people are sensitive to such common foods as milk, wheat, corn and nuts. They have been eating these foods for so long and so frequently that they don't make the connection between them and their symptoms. Food reactions can be very hard to pin down since they may occur instantly or several hours after the ingestion of a particular food. They can trigger a whole range of symptoms and they can wax and wane. Some food allergies worsen during times of great stress or they can be seasonal.

The one surefire way to find out whether you're allergic, intolerant or sensitive to a food is to eliminate it from your diet. After four days, reintroduce it. Your symptoms may reappear in a marked and obvious manner since your body has "deadapted" to the offending food. There will then be no doubt about whether you are allergic or not. The elimination diet is highly effective and should be overseen by your doctor. You need to be monitored carefully. In many cases, the food should be reintroduced in small amounts, as little as half a teaspoon, to prevent highly unpleasant reactions.

A JOURNEY TOWARD WELLNESS

I'm often struck by the unfortunate and unnecessary suffering that many people with mitral valve prolapse experience. In all too many cases, they have seen a number of medical professionals who often seem to contribute to the suffering rather than to alleviate it. I offer the following story because it is typical of what many of my patients have experienced and because it has a happy ending.

Josephine was a 28-year-old stockbroker involved in a very risky type of security product called "distressed securities." These were companies in bankruptcy or reorganization, and the idea was to identify hidden values for investors—obviously a stressful business. Nevertheless, Josephine did extremely well with this and was financially very successful. She managed her stress with regular visits to a health club where she worked out on the machines and used the Jacuzzi. And she followed what she thought was a good, healthy low-fat diet, with lots of salads, pasta and fruit juice. She also drank a cappucino with lunch and four or five diet colas a day.

Suddenly, out of the blue, she began to develop symptoms of extreme chest pressure to the point where she felt like she couldn't breathe. Actually, the first time this happened, a friend had taken her to the emergency room because Josephine thought she was dying. The resident reassured her that she wasn't having a heart attack and that nothing was basically wrong with her. In fact, the

ER staff seemed a little bit impatient with her, as if she were being hysterical over nothing.

Well, this threw her. Josephine was a very bright woman. She had to use her head and her gut instinct every day at her job, and her gut instinct told her that something was definitely wrong. She couldn't figure out why the doctors at the emergency room were so perfunctory and she was afraid of having another one of these attacks. She did have a few recurring episodes, though not as severe as the one that sent her to the hospital. She also was having trouble concentrating at work partly because she was worried about the chest symptoms, but sometimes for no apparent reason.

Josephine then went to her private physician who listened to her story, nodded knowingly and said, "Look, Jo, you're obviously taking it on the chin with stress. You had a panic attack, that's what we call it. You're chewing up more stress in a day at your job than most people deal with in a month. Take some time off, go lie on a beach, relax and get some perspective on this. There isn't anything wrong with you that a couple of weeks at Cancun can't fix. Everything checks out on your physical exam. Your electrocardiogram is normal—you don't have a heart problem. You do have a little bit of a heart murmur, but that's probably nothing. I think you'll be fine if you can get away from the stress for awhile. Don't let yourself get too worked up over this." Josephine had the distinct feeling that the doctor was trying to calm her down, and she kept wondering if this was all there was to it.

Jo did manage to schedule a vacation, but with a lingering feeling that something about her heart wasn't right. She remembered her doctor had said something about a heart murmur that she didn't quite understand, but she'd forgotten to ask exactly what that meant since all the talk was about stress. What's worse, she experienced a few more episodes of chest pressure while on vacation. She talked herself into the notion that they weren't dangerous this time, but they were alarming nonetheless. She was on vacation, hanging out at the beach, so where was the stress coming from?

When she came back, Josephine went to see a cardiologist. The cardiologist listened to her heart and expressed some concern. "You have a murmur," he said, "Let's do an echocardiogram." He went into another room while the technician performed the test. After Jo had dressed, he glanced at the test and said, "You have mitral valve prolapse." "What's that?" she asked fearfully. "It's not really significant," the cardiologist told her. "It's a benign type of murmur. A lot of people have this, and you don't need to worry about it. However, when you go to the dentist, you'll need to take antibiotics to prevent getting a heart infection from all the bacteria that's stirred up in your mouth." "But what about the chest pressure?" Jo asked. "You don't need to worry about that either," he said. "A lot of people with mitral valve prolapse have funny feelings in their chest. It's not medically significant. but I can see you're pretty anxious about this, so I'll give you a prescription for a beta-blocker—that seems to help a lot of my patients who have this."

Josephine started taking the medication, which seemed to reduce the frequency of the chest episodes but left her feeling groggy, tired and a little depressed. Her work began to suffer. She became anxious about the medication—she'd take it some days and not take it on others, while worrying that her heart might act up. And she kept having the spacey feelings with difficulty concentrating. She also backed off from her exercise program since she knew she had a "heart condition." Given what the cardiologist had told her, she thought it would be perilous.

At this point, Jo found herself becoming more and more anxious and at the same time depressed, so she consulted a psychiatrist. This was a "psychopharmacologist," one of a new breed of psychiatrists who dispense with the talking cure and offer the nostrums of advanced research in mood-altering medications. In fact, this was the only kind of psychiatry her health plan covered; it didn't cover weekly psychotherapy sessions. The doctor listened to her symptoms, which now included fatigue, anxiety, apprehension about her heart, continued chest pressure and shortness of breath, and told her, "You have a classic panic disorder." He explained that this was what he called a somatization disorder, and it meant she was taking her mental and emotional anxiety and giving it a physical location in her chest. The problem, he told her, was basically in her head, but there was a good prognosis for this because of new developments in psychopharmacology. He prescribed an antidepressant and an antianxiety medication and asked her to make an appointment to see him in two weeks. He did offer her the names of some psychologists in case she wanted to talk to someone but said the medication should fix her up.

Jo was now on three medications. The chest pressure was improved, but she felt drugged all the time. She had gained 20 pounds after giving up the health club and starting the medications and was feeling that she just couldn't cut it at work. People at the job told her she didn't look well. She had a lot of trouble concentrating and, when she finally came to see me, told me she really felt almost zombie-like.

Josephine came to see me because she thought that a nutritionally oriented doctor might help her with vitamins or her diet. When I first saw her I asked, "What are you eating?" She told me that since she had a heart problem she was being very careful about following a low-fat diet. I asked if the cardiologist had told her that mitral valve prolapse wasn't necessarily affected by cholesterol. She said no.

I suggested to her that an important test that might reveal something about her condition would be a glucose tolerance test to check her levels of blood sugar and how they varied in response to eating. She took the test, which revealed that her blood sugar was extremely low in the middle of the test. At this same point in the test, she reported the same symptoms of chest pressure that she'd originally had and the feelings of spaciness that seemed to be made worse by her medications. Measuring her levels of adrenaline at this point showed a tremendous outpouring of catecholamines; her own body chemistry was causing her symptoms. I also checked her magnesium levels and found them extremely low.

We then talked about her mitral valve prolapse. I explained it to her in detail, stressing that it was neither a cardiac condition nor something "in her head." It wasn't a "heart problem" in the sense that anything about her heart was causing her symptoms. I explained that her autonomic nervous system was askew and that, while job stress was a factor in her overall picture, it was not the cause of all her symptoms. In fact, I suggested that the challenging and exciting stress of her job was probably beneficial to her general vitality. Rather, a combination of factors had caused a meltdown of her autonomic stability. These included the mitral valve prolapse condition and the stress of her job plus her physical deconditioning since she'd given up her exercise program; internal stress from sugar, caffeine and her high-carbohydrate diet; and magnesium deficiency.

We got her to cut out the coffee, tea and cola drinks and got her started on a diet with more protein and fewer of the pastas and starchy foods that sent her blood sugar rocketing up and then crashing down. She started taking magnesium supplements, slowly got back into her exercise program and added a yoga class with breathing exercises and gentle stretching. We gradually weaned her off all the medications. Within six months, Josephine was back in charge of her life, impressing her clients at the office and no longer living in fear and anxiety. A major cognitive shift, along with some lifestyle adjustments, had freed her from a mysterious downward spiral.

THE MEDICAL CONTROVERSY OVER MVP

Conventional Medicine

Mitral valve prolapse is simply an anatomical abnormality of the heart and has been exaggerated as a syndrome. If you look at the general population you find that many people don't have mitral valve prolapse but have one or more of its symptoms.

People with a certain constellation of symptoms are actually suffering from somatization disorder, which is a psychiatric problem.

There is small but measurable risk of endocarditis associated with mitral valve prolapse, so prophylactic antibiotics should always be given to all MVP patients before every dental or surgical procedure. We don't need to be concerned about the effects of antibiotic use, which are minor.

Since MVP is not a serious health problem, there's no need to aggressively look for it or even necessarily to tell a patient he or she has it.

There may occasionally be some unpleasant symptoms associated with MVP, but the condition is not really treatable—all we can do is observe it. Don't start imagining symptoms just because you have this. If problems arise, antianxiety drugs or beta-blockers can be prescribed.

Holistic Medicine

Mitral valve prolapse is a complex syndrome involving disturbance of the autonomic nervous system. The actual valvular abnormality is just the tip of the iceberg and is an indicator of a constellation of symptoms.

People who have mitral valve prolapse and its symptoms are suffering from a real physical syndrome—it's not all in their heads.

Overuse of antibiotics is a growing health problem that contributes to emerging antibiotic resistance to many diseases, and to individual health problems such as *candida* infection. MVP patients should not all routinely be given prophylactic antibiotics before dental work unless a cardiologist has determined from an echocardiogram that backflow of blood in the heart is clearly shown.

People should always be informed if they have MVP and be told about the existence of the syndrome and the possible symptoms so they won't suffer needlessly.

You don't have to suffer needlessly—aggressive treatment with nutritional supplements, relaxation techniques, breathing training and exercise therapy can help you bring the symptoms under control. Most important to remember—it's not all in your head.

FOR FURTHER READING

Confronting Mitral Valve Prolapse Syndrome by Lyn Frederickson, M.S.N. Warner Books, 1992.